FIRST
SPORTS
SOURCE

FIRST SOURCE TO
HOCKEY

RULES, EQUIPMENT, AND KEY PLAYING TIPS

by Tyler Omoth

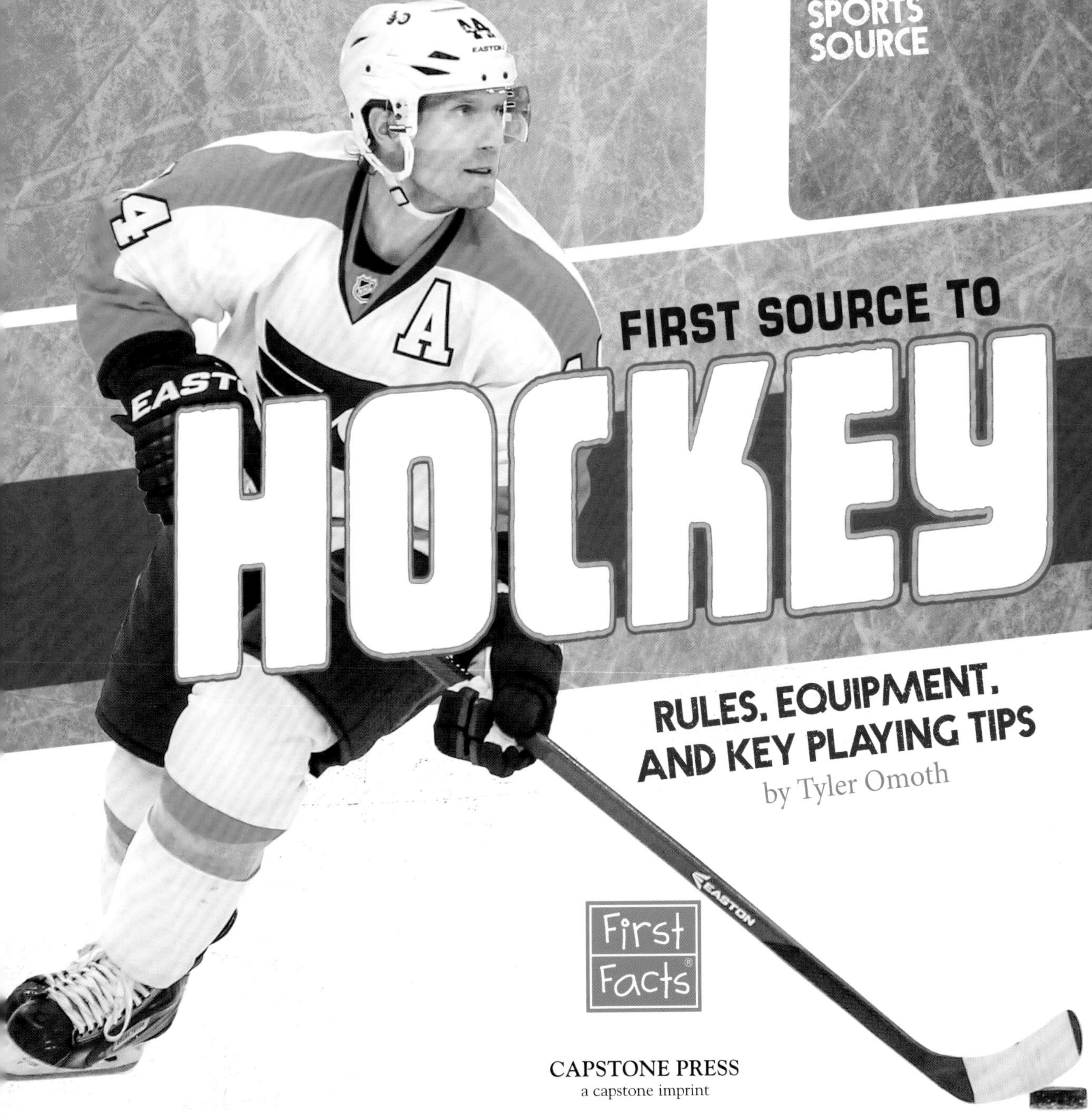

First
Facts®

CAPSTONE PRESS
a capstone imprint

First Facts are published by Capstone Press,
1710 Roe Crest Drive, North Mankato, Minnesota 56003
www.mycapstone.com

Library of Congress Cataloging-in-Publication Data

Cataloging-in-publication information is on file with the Library of Congress.
ISBN 978-1-4914-8423-4 (library binding)
ISBN 978-1-4914-8432-6 (paperback)
ISBN 978-1-4914-8427-2 (eBook PDF)

Editorial Credits
Mandy Robbins, editor; Heidi Thompson, designer; Eric Gohl, media researcher;
Lori Blackwell, production specialist

Photo Credits
Dreamstime: Jerry Coli, 7, Leszek Wrona, cover, Martin Ellis, 12, Twoegrets, 20 (bottom);
Newscom: Cal Sport Media/Billy Hurst, 11, Cal Sport Media/Danny Reise, 9, Cal Sport Media/
Kostas Lymperopoulos, 19, Icon SMI/Bill Streicher, 17, Icon SMI/Ric Tapia, 15, Icon Sportswire/
Jeanine Leech, 5; Shutterstock: Click Images, 21 (bottom), lsantilli, 20 (top), Iurii Osadchi, 13,
photosthatrock, 1, 21 (top)

Design Elements: Shutterstock

Printed and bound in China.
092015   009228S16

TABLE OF CONTENTS

Get In the Game!

National Hockey League (NHL) players glide across the ice with power and skill. Put on some skates and try hammering a **slap shot** like Pittsburgh Penguins star Sidney Crosby. If you like fast action on the ice, hockey is the sport for you.

"Every day is a great day for hockey."

–Mario Lemieux, former star player for the Pittsburg Penguins

ORIGINS OF HOCKEY

Basic forms of field hockey have been played for 4,000 years. The game is very popular in Europe. In the mid-1800s, Canadians made use of their cold climate and transferred the game onto the ice.

slap shot—the fastest and most forceful shot in hockey; a player raises his or her stick and slaps the puck hard toward the goal, putting his or her full body power behind it

SIDNEY CROSBY

FACT:
Ice hockey made its first appearance in the Olympic Games in 1924. Women's ice hockey was introduced to the Olympics in 1998.

CHAPTER 1
Ready to Play!

Equipment

The puck, hockey stick, and skates are the most basic pieces of hockey equipment. For safety, players wear helmets, visors, and a variety of pads. Goalies need extra padding and a protective mask for when a fast puck flies at them. They also have special sticks and big gloves to help block shots.

FACT:
Hockey pucks are made of **vulcanized** rubber. Before games, they are frozen to keep them from bouncing during play.

vulcanized—describes rubber that has been treated with heat and chemicals to make it stronger

The Hockey Rink

A hockey rink is almost rectangular. But it has rounded corners so the puck doesn't get stuck. A red line marks the center of the rink. A blue line on either side of the red line marks each team's **end zone**. The space between the blue lines is the **neutral zone**. Five circles mark spots for **face-offs**.

FACT:
Olympic hockey rinks are wider than North American hockey rinks. The blue lines are also farther apart, creating a larger neutral zone.

end zone—the area between the goal line and the end line at either end of a hockey rink
neutral zone—the area of a hockey rink that is between the two blue lines
face-off—when a player from each team battles for possession of the puck to start or restart play

The Goals

Hockey goals are built with metal pipes and white netting. A goal is 6 feet (1.8 meters) wide and 4 feet (1.2 m) tall. That seems like an easy shot until you put a goalie in there with his big pads, stick, and glove. A curved line in front of the goal marks the **crease**. Other players cannot shoot the puck from inside the goal crease.

FACT:
The ice in a NHL arena is kept at 16 degrees Fahrenheit (-8.9 degrees Celsius).

crease—the area directly in front of the goal in hockey; it's often painted blue

CHAPTER 2

How the Game Works

Hockey is played in three 20-minute periods. Each team can have six players on the ice. Substitutions can happen at any time. Players score goals by shooting the puck into the opponent's net. The team with the most goals at the end of the game wins.

THE STANLEY CUP

Hockey's highest prize, the Stanley Cup, is named after Lord Stanley of Preston. Stanley was a former Canadian Governor General. The Stanley Cup is given to the team that wins the NHL playoffs each year. Each player gets to spend a day with the Cup.

13

Get Into Position

Forwards focus on offense by shooting and passing the puck. Defensemen try to get the puck away from the other team. They want to keep opponents away from the goal. Each team has a goalie who stays near the goal. The goalie's job is to stop the other team from scoring.

PULLING THE GOALIE

Goalies are no help on offense. They're not even allowed to touch the puck on the opposing team's side of the rink. When teams need to score a goal toward the end of a game, they often bench the goalie to put in an extra skater.

FORWARD

Shooting

There are four main ways to take a shot on goal. They are slap shots, **wrist shots**, **backhands**, and **snapshots**. Players try different types of shots depending on their position to the goal. Skaters often make quick passes to one another near the goal. Quick passing often leads to open shots as the goalie moves back and forth.

FACT:
Hockey skates have shorter, more curved blades than figure skates. The special blades help hockey players build up speed quickly.

wrist shot—a type of shot in which a player uses his or her wrists to quickly snap the stick and shoot the puck
backhand—a shot or pass in which the player uses the back side of the stick's blade
snapshot—a short, quick shot used just as a pass is received using little to no backswing

16

CHAPTER 3
Rules of the Game

Referees enforce the rules of the game. Players who break the rules can end up in the penalty box. They may even get thrown out of the game. A player's punishment depends on how serious the offense was. Minor penalties usually get 2 minutes in the box. Major penalties can get up to 10 minutes.

FACT:
College hockey has a playoff tournament that begins with 16 teams. The tournament is nicknamed "The Frozen Four."

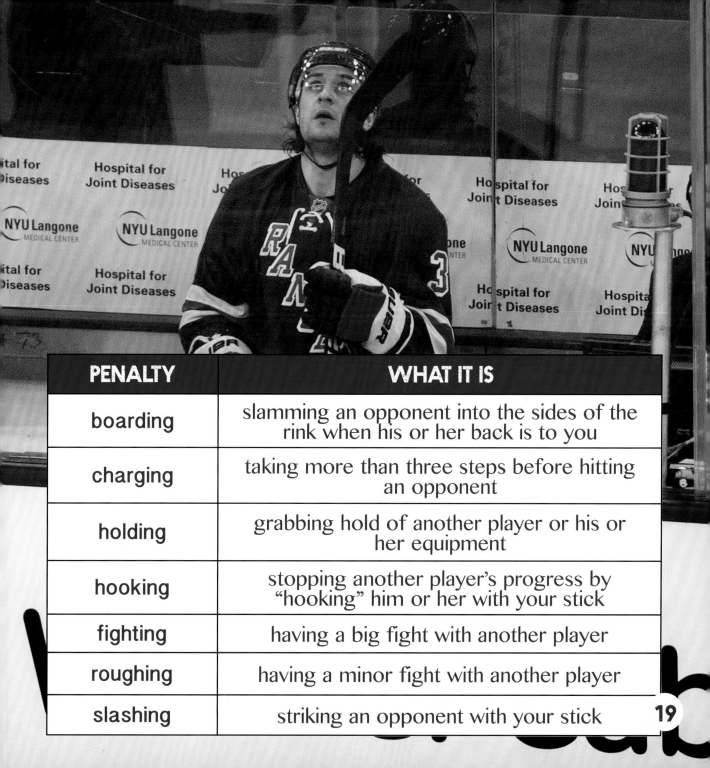

PENALTY	WHAT IT IS
boarding	slamming an opponent into the sides of the rink when his or her back is to you
charging	taking more than three steps before hitting an opponent
holding	grabbing hold of another player or his or her equipment
hooking	stopping another player's progress by "hooking" him or her with your stick
fighting	having a big fight with another player
roughing	having a minor fight with another player
slashing	striking an opponent with your stick

CHAPTER 4
Playing Tips

Now that you know the basics of ice hockey, it's time to start practicing! Here are some tips to get you started.

SHOOTING

The wrist shot is the most important shot to master. Practice shooting pucks at an empty goal to sharpen your skills.

FACT

Russian hockey skater Denis Kulyash holds the record for the fastest hockey shot. He hit a puck at an astonishing 110.3 miles (177.5 kilometers) per hour.

PASSING

When receiving a pass, let your stick drift backward with the puck just a little. This is called "cushioning the puck."

GOALTENDING

Always keep your eye on the puck, even when it's on the other side of the rink. A long shot could come your way.

SKATING

For better balance on the ice, bend your knees deeply while skating. When you push forward, fully extend your legs and ankles to build up speed.

"It's not necessarily the amount of time you spend at practice that counts; it's what you put into the practice."

-Eric Lindros,
former NHL forward

Glossary

backhand (BAK-hand)—a shot or pass in which the player uses the back side of the stick's blade

crease (KREES)—the area directly in front of the goal in hockey; it's often painted blue

end zone (END ZOHN)—the area between the goal line and the end line at either end of a hockey rink

face-off (FAYSS-awf)—when a player from each team battles for possession of the puck to start or restart play

neutral zone (NOO-truhl ZOHN)—the area of a hockey rink that is between the two blue lines

penalty box (PEN-uhl-tee BOX)—an enclosed space next to the rink where penalized players sit for a specific length of time

slap shot (SLAP SHOT)—the fastest and most forceful shot in the game; a player raises his or her stick and slaps the puck hard toward the goal, putting his or her full body power behind it

snapshot (SNAP-shot)—a short, quick shot used just as a pass is received using little to no backswing

vulcanized (VUHL-kuh-nyzed)—describes rubber that has been treated with heat and chemicals to make it stronger

wrist shot (RIST SHOT)—a type of shot in which a player uses his or her wrists to quickly snap the stick and shoot the puck

Read More

Doeden, Matt. *All About Hockey*. All About Sports. North Mankato, Minn.: Capstone Press, 2015.

Hurley, Michael. *Ice Hockey*. Fantastic Sports Facts. Chicago: Capstone Raintree, 2013.

Morey, Allen. *Hockey*. I Love Sports. Minneapolis: Jump!, 2015.

Internet Sites

FactHound offers a safe, fun way to find Internet sites related to this book. All of the sites on FactHound have been researched by our staff.

Here's all you do:

Visit www.facthound.com

Type in this code: 9781491484234

Super-cool stuff! Check out projects, games and lots more at **www.capstonekids.com**

Index